Bingham's Missouri

All the George Caleb Bingham drawings in this exhibition are from the collection owned by the Mercantile Library of St. Louis. They are presently for sale by the Library, which has loaned them for this exhibition in seven Missouri cities.

Many Missourians, concerned at the likelihood that the collection would be broken up and widely scattered, have joined the effort by Bingham Sketches, Inc., a not-for-profit organization formed by the Governor, to purchase this important collection and maintain it as a Missouri cultural treasure.

A statewide citizens committee, appointed by the Governor, has launched a public subscription drive to raise $1.8 million in cash and three-year pledges by June 1976 to acquire the drawings. The Nelson Gallery-Atkins Museum, Kansas City, and the St. Louis Art Museum have offered to serve as repositories for the collection under controlled conditions of heat, humidity and lighting.

All contributions are tax-deductible, and may be mailed to Governor Christopher S. Bond, Jefferson City, Mo. 65101.

This exhibition is sponsored by The Missouri State Council on the Arts and the National Endowment for the Arts

Exhibition Schedule

Kansas City
Nelson Gallery—Atkins Museum
September 26 - October 26

St. Louis
St. Louis Art Museum
November 14 - January 4

Springfield
Springfield Art Museum
January 11 - January 21

Cape Girardeau
Kent Library, Southeast Missouri
State University
January 31 - February 7

Columbia
Museum of Art and Archaeology, in
Ellis Library, University of Missouri
   and
State Historical Society of Missouri
February 13 - March 7

Hannibal
Mark Twain Museum
March 1 - March 7

St. Joseph
Albrecht Gallery and Museum of Art
April 1 - April 11

Cover drawing: *Stump Speaker*, believed to have been an unused study for the lost painting, *The Stump Orator*, of 1847

Mercantile Library Collection

Concurrent Activities

A Package Exhibition of Reproductions from original Bingham drawings and one of his paintings is available to interested organizations. There are no special security requirements for this exhibition. It could be hung in a public library, a shopping center, a club house, bank or any public place. Write Bingham Sketches, Inc., P. O. Box 720, Jefferson City, Mo., 65101 for reservation.

Speaker Service and Slide Presentation available to schools and clubs. To schedule a speaker, call one of the museums exhibiting *Bingham's Missouri*. This service is provided by The Junior League of St. Louis and Kansas City, the Service League of Springfield, and other clubs in Missouri.

Bingham's Missouri

Some states are fortunate enough to have been the home of artists who saw clearly, and remembered well, and continued to be stimulated by the surroundings they had known while growing up. The odds are against this, because an artist is more likely to find his home grounds unexciting, unprofitable and conducive to a provincial confinement of his vision.

An imposing roster of painters, sculptors, novelists, playwrights and musicians have been *from* Missouri, and a rare few have been *of* Missouri—practicing their art here, and imbuing it with the special flavor of this heartland region. We have reason to be grateful for the artists' perceptions that reveal to us something of our own historic identity, an identity that is as varied as the range of topography from the Osage Plains to the ancient St. Francois Mountains.

George Caleb Bingham was such an artist, the first Missouri artist to attempt an interpretation of the place where he lived and the people he knew. The historic identity that he presents is that of his home territory, Central Missouri in the early years of statehood, with its constant river traffic and its towns that grew from boat landings. His views of life on the rivers and in the towns are straightforward and unromanticized. He presents his fellow citizens with sensitivity and wit, not idealized and never satirized. These are the people who settled that country,

and went on from his boyhood towns of Franklin and Arrow Rock to establish the Santa Fe Trail. We see them now just as he saw them then, and just as they saw each other, in the paintings that were his best work.

The drawings in this exhibition were his preparation for these paintings; the character studies that were integrated into the communions of flatboat crews floating on the silent rivers, and of large turn-outs in the courthouse squares. They are works of art in their own right, and uniquely a part of the Missouri heritage.

George Caleb Bingham

Bingham was self-trained as an artist, and was educated otherwise by his mother and his own wide reading. It was not until his twenty-fourth year that he traveled outside central Missouri, but after that he ranged energetically through the eastern and southern United States, and parts of Europe. Portraits were his bread-and-butter work; his great period of river paintings, the election series and other genre was the 12 years from 1845 to 1857. Political activity after the Civil War made heavy demands on his time, to the detriment of his art. Within a few years after his death in 1879 he was almost forgotten outside Missouri. The Bingham revival is largely owed to a series of thorough studies of his career and work, beginning with Fern Helen Rusk in 1917, and extended by Albert Christ-Janer in 1940 and this year. The first full publication of the Mercantile Library drawings by John Francis McDermott, in 1959, was followed by several national exhibitions of the drawings and some paintings. The first critical study of Bingham's art, with a catalogue raisonne, by E. Maurice Bloch in 1967, confirmed Bingham's position in the peerage of significant American artists.

George Caleb Bingham was born March 20, 1811, on a farm west of Charlottesville, Virginia, in the Blue Ridge Mountains. His father, Henry Vest Bingham, was a Methodist preacher and farmer. He was married in 1808 to Mary Amend, the daughter of a German miller, Matthias Amend, who gave his farm and mill to his daughter as a wedding present. He made his home with the Binghams, and Henry Bingham raised tobacco on this farm until he lost the property through the default of a friend's note for which he had been surety.

In 1819 the family, including Amend, moved to Franklin, Missouri, a new town on the north side of the Missouri River a short distance upstream and across the river from Boonville. George Caleb Bingham was then eight years of age. He had one older brother, two younger brothers and two younger sisters. Two other children were born in Missouri.

Franklin had been platted only three years before, and already was booming. It was the seat of the northwestern quadrant of Missouri, and was second to St. Louis in the territory's business volume.

The Boon's Lick Country has a reputation for fertile soil and good prospects. There was a legendary saying that "If you plant a tenpenny nail there at night, hit'll sprout crow bars by mornin'." Families from Tennessee,

The Bingham House, Arrow Rock, which he had built in 1837. His mother occupied it until her death. Later owners enlarged it, and it was restored in 1936 and 1965. (George McCue photo). Below, portion of review of a studio exhibition of portraits, in *Missouri Intelligencer*, Columbia, March 14, 1835. (State Historical Society of Missouri, Columbia.)

Missouri Intelligencer.

COLUMBIA;
Saturday, March 14, 1835.

THE FINE ARTS.—We cannot refrain from expressing our delight, occasioned by a visit, a few mornings since, to the portrait-room of Mr. Bingham, upon Guitar street. Upon entering, our sensations partook more of the nature of surprise, than of any other emotion. A collection of well finished portraits each affording full evidence of a cultivated mimetic skill, and of an undoubted high creative genius - is a circumstance, that deserves a place as an important era, in the history of Trans-Mississippian progress, towards a state of intellectual and social refinement.

George Caleb Bingham

The St. Louis levee, as Bingham knew it late in life. Studio rooms that he rented were in the vicinity of Main and Market streets, lower left.

(From *Pictorial St. Louis*, by Camille N. Dry and Rich J. Compton, 1875)

Kentucky and Virginia were arriving every day in "Immense numbers of waggons, carriages, carts, etc.," as the town's newly established newspaper, the *Missouri Intelligencer and Boon's Lick Advertiser*, reported. *The St. Louis Enquirer* had noted west-bound traffic of about 20 conveyances a week through St. Charles "with wealthy, respectable emigrants from various states." Some, not wealthy, were coming up from southern Missouri. Because of earthquakes in the New Madrid area, Congress had issued certificates in 1815 to displaced settlers of that region for land in the Boon's Lick Country.

Franklin soon had good schools, a library, a General Land Office and well-stocked stores; it had Dr. John Sappington, who discovered the efficacy of quinine in treating malaria, and John Hardeman, a non-practicing lawyer who laid out a botanical garden. It even had a jockey club.

Henry Bingham opened a tavern at Franklin "at the sign of the Square and Compass," the *Intelligencer* informed its subscribers, and became a partner with William Lamme in a chewing tobacco and cigar-making business. He bought 160 acres of farm land in the newly founded Saline County, near where Arrow Rock was platted a few years later.

Matthias Amend seems to have lived on the farm until his death by drowning in the river. Henry Bingham died in 1823, when he was 40, and his widow had to sell household goods to pay claims against his estate. The tobacco factory interest was lost, and she moved with her children to the Arrow Rock farm.

As a child, George Caleb Bingham had shown aptitude for drawing, which he practiced by copying engraved reproductions of paintings and other art— just as many another American artist had groped his way into the study of form, modeling, perspective, tonalities and composition. His father's death when he was 12 interrupted even this, since he was needed to help work on the farm. His health was not equal to this, and he became apprenticed to a Boonville cabinetmaker. An early intention to study law evaporated when an itinerant portrait-painter came to town. Bingham later emphasized that he had never seen a portrait painted except for those done by himself, so it appears that the itinerant did not permit any looking over his shoulder to learn whatever limited techniques he may have had. His visit, however, renewed Bingham's zeal to know more about painting.

When he was 22, and had attracted some attention by painting signs and by practice work that he had shown, four young friends at Arrow Rock offered to sit for portraits, which he executed with house paint and stumps of brushes abandoned by the itinerant artist. It is not known what became of these pictures. His earliest known portraits were done the next year, 1834, when he carried out a number of commissions in Boonville and Columbia. They included Dr. and Mrs. John Sappington; Meredith Miles Marmaduke, who became Governor 10 years later, and James S. Rollins, with whom Bingham developed a warm friendship.

Bingham pulled himself along through many an awkwardness before his portrait figures began to breathe and be at ease in their picture space. But even his first portraits had a forceful individuality that takes them completely out of the class of the naive painting of folk art. The first critical review of his work, in the *Missouri Intelligencer*, Columbia, in 1835, gently urged that "the pencil of our artist, might be permitted occasionally, a stroke or two of flattery, with advantage. In some instances too faithful a copy of features is unfavorable in effect."

Although portraits were his livelihood, Bingham did not, in the thousand or so commissions of his lifetime, depart from the practice of painting what he saw, double-chins and all. In his own self-portraits, he shows the not quite perfect fit of a wig that he wore after a severe illness caused the loss of his hair. The subject who wore a dour expression to the sitting got a dour portrait.

In the highest tradition of portraiture, however, he achieved expressive characterization, even in the early years of an

George Caleb Bingham

invariable rigid positioning in a three-quarters view facing the viewer's left, and with an invariable little highlight at the tip of the nose. At first Bingham avoided hands. In 1835 he permitted himself a thumb, protruding from between the lapels of Colonel John Thornton's coat with the rest of the hand tucked inside. After another year or two, he began painting hands on women subjects, but they remained embryonic for some time longer.

It took longer still for Bingham to feel his way into a color equilibrium. He had early practice in tonalities from the study of monotone engravings, but his mature color came only after exposure to the work of skilled painters in extensive travels. An 1849 biographical sketch said that although he was "in total darkness in regard to color, his drawing generally gave so strong a likeness" that his patrons were pleased.

The St. Louis levee, 1848, with densely moored steamboats and a forest of tall stacks. (Missouri Historical Society, St. Louis)

Ross E. Taggart, chief curator of the Nelson Gallery-Atkins Museum, Kansas City, wrote in *The Art Quarterly* in 1944: "One of the most typical of his chromatic idiosyncracies is the use of an almost transparent red in the shadows . . . most noticeable in his portraits, whether they were painted as early as 1834, or as late as 1877. This luminous, hot red shadow is most apparent under the nose and around the ears and hands. In strong contrast is the painting of cool, greenish half-lights in the flesh tones. This strange opposition of warm shadows, cool half-lights, and warm high-lights fills the color with a vibrant energy and is so personal with Bingham as to amount almost to a signature." Taggart analyzed Bingham's palette as "muted off-shades, blue-greens, sage-greens, plums, cerises and cool pinks." This unorthodox scheme was, however, "carefully ordered and sensitively related."

Following a friendly and profitable reception at Columbia, where his usual fee was $25 a portrait, Bingham opened a studio in St. Louis in March, 1834, and invited business with a professional card in the *Missouri Republican*. This studio was on "Market St., opposite the Shepherd of the Valley Printing Office (upstairs)." On numerous future sojourns, Bingham favored this part of the business district, near the courthouse (a small two-story brick building in the block now occupied by the later domed building known as the Old Courthouse), and convenient to the levee.

At that time the church now known as the Old Cathedral was the new Cathedral, on Walnut east of Third Street. Leon Pomarede, a Parisian emigre artist, had just finished its interior decoration, including transparencies painted on the clear glass

Self-Portrait, 1834-1835   Oil on canvas, 28 x 22½   St. Louis Art Museum

windows, and an altarpiece "after Rubens." It is not unreasonable to suppose that Bingham might have received at least some technical suggestions from Pomarede, who later gave lessons to Carl Wimar, the painter of Western Indian themes and of the murals in the Old Courthouse dome. St. Louis was well past its first half-century by then, and a number of its families had selections of recent American art and copies of old masters that Bingham could have viewed as a beginning of his studies of work by other artists to advance his own skill.

His prices soon went up to $40 or $50 a portrait, and on a third visit to St. Louis in 1836 he had enough work to occupy two months. Then he went back to Boonville, and was married to Elizabeth Hutchison, daughter of an early settler of Franklin. In July, 1837, they bought a lot in Arrow Rock and

The Dull Story, 1843-1844   Oil on canvas, 50⅜ x 38⅞   St. Louis Art Museum

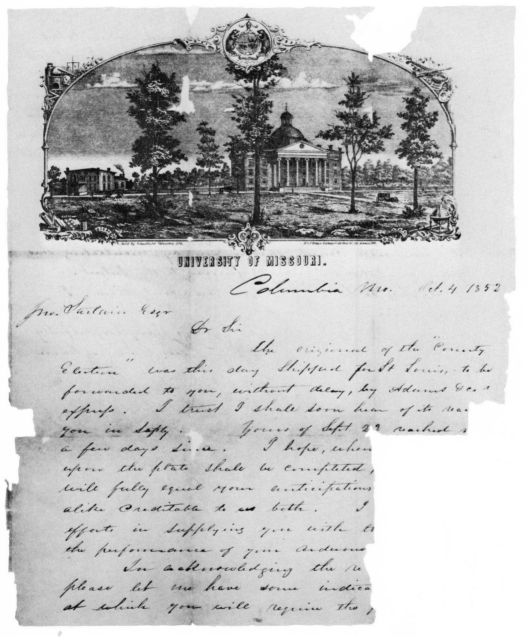

Portion of letter from Bingham to his engraver,
John Sartain about shipment of *County Election*,
October 4, 1852. Missouri Historical Society,
St. Louis.

built the little brick house where the artist's mother lived for the rest of her life.

By this time Bingham had gone as far as Natchez to paint portraits, and he was eager to visit Philadelphia. The Pennsylvania Academy of Fine Arts, founded in 1805, housed America's first art museum and one of its first art schools.

There, in 1838, he enjoyed his first visit to a professional art exhibition at the Academy, it is presumed. He did not keep a journal or other evidence of his experience, but the Academy was having its annual show at the time, and his first drawings—some nude sketches from the antique—could have been done from one of the gallery's seven Venuses.

Bingham seems to have gone on to New York, for in the following October the Apollo Gallery there exhibited—an indication of prior contact—his first recorded genre painting, *Western Boatmen Ashore*. No description has been found of this lost predecessor of the river series. He continued to solicit portraits, which he candidly referred to as "potboilers," but several paintings of 1843-1844 give evidence of transition into more eventful themes. Gallery visitors and reviewers over the country generally were becoming restive about the sameness of portrait exhibitions, and the artist in Bingham obviously needed a greater challenge.

George Caleb Bingham

He moved back and forth in Missouri on portrait business. While maintaining studios at various St. Louis locations, always in the area of Market Street near the river, he made several trips back to his home territory. During one of these a St. Louis studio that he shared with another artist burned, destroying a number of portraits.

He sent six paintings to an exhibition at the National Academy of Design, New York, all of them beginnings of his new interest. Two were figures with non-portrait titles, two were anecdotal illustrations from Robert Burns's "Tam O'Shanter," one was a landscape, and the sixth was *Pennsylvania Farmer*. It is not known whether they still exist.

Another intimation of a future activity —political campaigning—came in the spring of 1840, when he painted a banner for the Saline County delegation to the Whig convention at Rocheport, a few miles down the river from Boonville, held in June. It was a banner to be viewed from all directions, painted on a four-sided canvas frame, each panel six feet square. It included a life-size portrait of General William Henry Harrison, the Whig Presidential candidate, on a marble pedestal, and the other spaces were filled with scenes of commerce, agriculture and military exploits, and with mottoes, the flag and a western landscape with the sun breaking through distant clouds. It stirred enthusiastic comment.

That fall, at the age of 39, he went to Washington, D.C., accompanied by his wife. They lived in a boarding house on Pennsylvania Avenue, immediately west of the railroad station that then stood at the foot of Capitol Hill. Bingham had a studio room in the Capitol basement, and he went in pursuit of prestigious portrait business while also cultivating his abilities at the kind of pictures that he believed would please a larger public.

The Dull story is a stage of his transition into genre, for although the young woman who is shown charmingly asleep in a chair with a magazine in her lap was the artist's wife, she is more a model than an individual. The effort is directed at creating a mood rather than a likeness, and the luscious, decorative colors depart from his customary portrait palette. This painting displays a well-advanced facility with textures, from the flesh like tinted marble to the satiny gown and the heavy material of the chair cushion. This and a painting of his little sleeping son, Horace, which is more an exercise in patterns and light effects than a portrait, are believed to have been done in Washington. Horace was born there March 13, 1841, on the same day that the Binghams's first child, four-year-old Newton, died of croup.

Whig party campaign badge for convention at Rocheport, June 3, 1844, for which Bingham painted a four-sided banner and was a delegate. (State Historical Society of Missouri, Columbia)

Bingham's studio, Kansas City, in 1870. His first *Order No. 11*, 1865-1868, which was in his estate inventory, leans against the wall. It is now owned by the Cincinnati Art Museum; the State Historical Society of Missouri, Columbia, has the second *Order No. 11*, of 1870. The other big painting is *Washington Crossing the Delaware*, 1856-1871. (John Francis McDermott)

Bingham remained in Washington for four years. There are three known surviving portraits of that time. A small likeness, on a panel, of John Quincy Adams, then (1844) a Representative in Congress, was given to James S. Rollins; two other versions were painted about six years later. An oil on canvas of Daniel Webster was given by Bingham to a Washington friend, Charles Wilkes, was later owned by Evelyn Walsh McLean and is now in the Thomas Gilcrease Institute of American History and Art, Tulsa, Oklahoma. A water color, 9 by 7 inches, of John Howard Payne, the composer of "Home, Sweet Home," was kept by the artist and was sold for $22.50 in an administrator's sale of his estate. This, Bingham's only known water color painting, is now owned by the St. Louis Mercantile Library Association. Portraits of a number of personages have been said to be among Bingham's Washington production—Henry Clay, Andrew Jackson, John C. Calhoun, James Buchanan and Martin van Buren among others— but there is no record of them. He may have made studies of more subjects than he painted, as the basis for such later portraits as Clay and Jackson in the Missouri Capitol.

A great many of his thousand or so portraits are still unaccounted for. Some are hanging unrecognized in living rooms, some are languishing in attics, and some were destroyed. Several important works were discovered in recent years.

Life on Missouri's Rivers

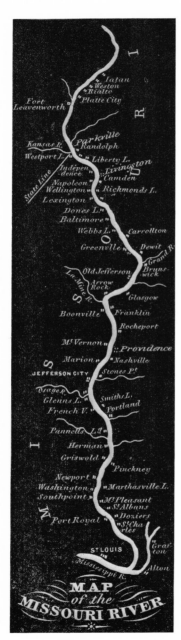

Early schematic diagram of Missouri River steamboat landings. Kansas City, so-named in 1853, is still "Westport L." on this chart. (Missouri Historical Society, St. Louis)

Missouri is the only state traversed by the nation's two principal rivers, which flow in parallel channels for several miles before they are joined above St. Louis. The Mississippi and Missouri river channels have determined the location of every city and town along their banks, sometimes misleadingly.

Franklin flourished briefly as the chief outfitting point for travelers over the Santa Fe trail, but cheap steamboat transportation moved the outfitting to Independence and Westport, which grew into Kansas City. The seat of Howard County was moved to Fayette, and the town of New Franklin was established in 1828 on higher and safer ground than Old Franklin which, within a few years, vanished almost without a trace.

For most of his years of back-and-forth travel across Missouri, Bingham rode steamboats. The *Zebulon M. Pike*, built in Kentucky, was the first to reach St. Louis in 1817. In 1819 the *Independence* made the first passage up the Missouri River from St. Louis to a point beyond Franklin and back in 21 days. That was the year in which Henry Bingham moved his famliy to Franklin.

When the Missouri River channel and steamboats had been improved, normal travel time from St. Louis to Jefferson City was 24 hours, with Boonville about another day farther west. At the river towns, the boats transferred passengers and freight, but they also had to stop at wood yard landings to take on fuel. Another source of fuel for the boilers and the cooking ranges was the wood boats, which waited here and there, ready to pull alongside with their loads so the big boats could stay safely in the channel. This was income for backwoods settlers, but between steamboats they had long waits with time for story-telling, card-playing, whisky-drinking and for jigging to a fiddle and the rhythm of knuckles thumping a frying pan.

The Missouri River was the interstate highway to the West. From the distant fur country came flatboats, dugouts and rafts loaded with beaver pelts and buffalo hides, and manned by shaggy men eager for the riverfront saloons in St. Louis.

All this was as much a part of the river scene as the sunrises and sunsets, and from the deck of many a steamboat to both sides of the state (it was 1865 before there was train service between St. Louis and Kansas City), Bingham could both see it and be a part of it.

Bingham's contemporaries who painted the American West—Carl Wimar, Alfred Jacob Miller, Charles Bodmer, George Catlin and others—passed through these scenes on their way from St. Louis to the more exotic genre of the vanishing Indian, on whom their faculties were concentrated. Although Indians were part of the river traffic, and in his youth had encampments in

River traffic at Weston, in northwest Missouri, a flourishing shipping point for tobacco and hemp for 20 years until the Missouri River channel shifted in 1857 and left it stranded.

The 1842 Missouri Capitol that Bingham knew at Jefferson City. It burned in 1911. The other building is Lohman's Landing, a tavern and warehouse, still standing and now being restored.

Barrels, boxes and bales on the St. Louis levee, with a flat boat and a raft edging through the lane of steamboats. From an 1870 banknote. (All, Missouri Historical Society, St. Louis)

Life on Missouri's Rivers

Saline County, Bingham had no close contact with them and barely touched on them as subject matter. He never traveled west of Kansas City. In keeping his focus on the scenes that he knew intimately, and on the people he understood, he created an inimitable record of Missouri's early years, and of ways of life that were disappearing even while he was painting them.

By this time Bingham's contacts with other artists could have helped him to realize how much a portfolio of sketches and drawings serves as reference material, especially for large compositions from many recollections and impressions. In the 1840s he began systematically making drawings, and those in this exhibition are studies that he did in pencil, brush, ink and gray wash heightened with white in preparation for the peak of his artistic achievement, the paintings of life on the rivers and in the river towns.

The St. Louis Mercantile Library Association has owned the drawings since 1868, when they were presented by John How, a former mayor and then president of the O'Fallon Polytechnic Institute. He had purchased from Bingham the three subjects in the Election Series and the *Jolly Flatboatmen in Port*. It is not known how he came into possession of the drawings, which had been mounted in a scrapbook.

The first publication of the entire set was in 1959, in John Francis

Nothing But a Crow, Harper's Weekly, 1868

McDermott's *George Caleb Bingham: River Portraitist*. This created public interest in a showing of the drawings, and in 1963 they were exhibited with some paintings at the M. Knoedler and Company Galleries, New York.

When the drawings were removed from the scrapbook for framing, nearly half of them were found to have figure details on the reverse sides.

The Trapper's Return, from sketch by A. Wilson

The drawing of the trapper in *Fur Traders Descending the Missouri*, was on the first page of the scrapbook, with the boy next.

Beaver Hut, after drawing by Charles Bodmer

At the western end of the St. Louis-fur country axis, the trappers lived in the wilds, gathering pelts during the winter for sale to traders at the spring rendezvous. Then came the long Missouri River voyage to the St. Louis markets. Pictures of life in this far-off region fascinated eastern magazine readers, and editors did their best to meet the demand.
(All, Missouri Historical Society, St. Louis)

Fur Traders Descending the Missouri, 1845

Oil on canvas, 29¼ x 36¼

The Metropolitan Museum of Art (Morris K. Jessup Fund, 1933)

Life on Missouri's Rivers

Fur Traders Descending the Missouri, Bingham's first important genre painting, was done in 1845 (the same year, as it happened, that the Mercantile Library was organized). Bingham submitted it to the American Art-Union, New York, an outgrowth of the Apollo Gallery where he had first exhibited. The Art-Union's purpose was to "foster American art" by buying paintings that it exhibited and then awarded among its members at an annual drawing. For their $5 dues all members received an engraving made from a selected painting. This arrangement opened up a regular market and national exposure for many artists, and it enlarged Bingham's reputation for the next decade. The Art-Union paid Bingham $150 for four paintings in 1845, of which $75 was for *Fur Traders.* It was awarded to Robert S. Bunker, of Mobile, Alabama, and descended in his family until the Metropolitan Museum of Art acquired it in 1933.

Detail from *Fur Traders Descending the Missouri*

The fur trader of Bingham's drawing is done with masterful authority, and it shows what a distance he had gone from his early brittle portraits. In the painting the trader is given a growth of beard, and his surly expression is intensified by the left-side shadow. The cut of his shirt is modified, and its pattern, like that of the boy's shirt, is visible in the river mist with startling clarity. It was some paintings later before Bingham mastered the blending of figures into their atmosphere. The animal tied in the bow has been variously identified as a fox, a bear cub and a cat.

Mercantile Library Collection

The study for the boy in *Fur Traders* shows him more touseled than in the painting, and his shirt realistically rumpled. The drawing details were more literally applied in a second version of this painting, *Trappers' Return* (1851), now at the Detroit Institute of Arts. McDermott estimates that there must have been about as many more drawings as the number now accounted for.

Mercantile Library Collection

Raftsmen Playing Cards, 1847   Oil on canvas, 28 x 36   St. Louis Art Museum

Life on Missouri's Rivers

By the time that Bingham did *Raftsmen Playing Cards* in 1847 his market value had gone up. The Art-Union paid $300 for it, unframed, and awarded it to an Albany, New York, editor, Edwin Croswell. The card game was identified by a reviewer as "three-up." A discerning reviewer in the *Missouri Republican* wrote: "He has not sought out those incidents or occasions which might be supposed to give the best opportunity for display, and a flashy, highly colored picture; but he has taken the simplest, most frequent and common occurences on our rivers—such as every boatman will encounter in a season—such as would seem, even to the casual and careless observer, of very ordinary moment, but which are precisely those in which the full and undisguised character of the boatman is displayed." When the painting was removed from its stretcher for cleaning at the St. Louis Art Museum, it was found that several inches of the landscape and the end of the plank on the right side had been folded under for framing. A second version of 1851, with four figures, is owned by the Right Reverend Paul Moore Jr., Washington, D.C.

Detail from *Raftsmen Playing Cards*

Bingham consistently built his large compositions in the classical pyramid. The two main actors in *Raftsmen* fit into this structure, and the outer figures establish its base line. The result is a compact grouping that focuses on the central characters and reinforces the idea of a vignette of human activity in the vast openness of the river landscape. Bingham makes the most of the immediate moment: In the sweeping view of wild countryside, the big question is whether the man studying his cards can best his opponent's ace.

The lesser figures in *Raftsmen* are as
carefully studied as the central ones.
They are subordinate to the theme, but
they participate significantly in the
manner of its presentation.

Mercantile Library Collection

Watching the Cargo, 1849   Oil on canvas, 26 x 36   State Historical Society of
Missouri, Columbia

Life on Missouri's Rivers

In *Life On the Mississippi* Mark Twain
wrote of the steamboat pilot's need to
know every bend in more than 1,000
miles of river, upstream and down, but
also to be able to ''read'' its surface
ripples for signs of new obstructions.
The shallower Missouri River had an
elusive channel, often constricted by
sandbars just under the surface. Pilots
would say that when the water stage
was low, navigation was ''like putting
a steamer on dry land, and sending a
boy ahead with a sprinkling pot.''
When a boat could not loosen the grip
of a sandbar, the next step was to
lighten it by removing some of the
cargo. That has been done here, with
three crew members preparing to
spend the night guarding a pile of
freight. The painting shows a highly
developed control of light, shadow,
massing and texture.

Detail from *Watching the Cargo*

The two dominant figures in *Watching the Cargo* were carefully studied in the drawings, which Bloch ranks "among the most powerful drawings in the collection." In these, he says, Bingham showed his "ability to translate his designs from the graphic to the oil medium without losing any of the force and character of the original."

Mercantile Library Collection

Bingham's drawings not only present clear, strong characterizations but also record the details of apparel so explicitly that his drawings constitute a reference library of how the shirts, jackets and pants of early Missouri men were cut and sewed. He shows several varieties of the stocking cap, such as this crewman is wearing. The sleeves of his loosely fitted pullover shirt are attached below the shoulders. The boots resemble today's casual footwear.

Mercantile Library Collection

Jolly Flatboatmen in Port, 1857   Oil on canvas, 47½ x 69½   St. Louis Art Museum

Life on Missouri's Rivers

There are three known paintings of the "Jolly Flatboatmen" theme, and possibly another that is unaccounted for. The first, done in 1846, was purchased by the Art-Union for $290, including frame, and was awarded to a New York grocer. For years it was known only through an engraved copy distributed by the Art-Union and published reproductions. This painting caused Bingham to be known as "The Missouri Artist." It was "discovered" in the collection of United States Senator Claiborne Pell, whose family had owned it for more than a half-century. A second version of about two years later is in a Kansas City collection. *Jolly Flatboatmen in Port* was painted on a visit to Duesseldorf in 1957. It shows the boat at the St. Louis levee, with the crew and visitors relaxing after unloading the cargo. Bingham loaned the painting to the Mercantile Library, then it was purchased by John How (who later presented the drawings), and passed into the hands of John H. Beach who gave it to the Library. The St. Louis Art Museum had it on loan for 10 years before purchasing it in 1944.

Detail from *Jolly Flatboatmen in Port*

Bingham made good use of his sketch book for this painting, done far from the scene and involving 20 figures. Some figures are new, others reworked from earlier paintings. He shows more of the fiddler's face in *Jolly Flatboatmen in Port* drawing at left, and displays a better understanding of how a fiddle is held and bowed than in the drawing, right, done for the painting of 1846. Details of the half-barrel, used for a seat, show clearly how the staves were bound.

Even though the pan-thumper was little changed from the previous versions, he was painted from a new drawing, given a different hat and longer sleeves. There is no drawing in the collection for the dancing man, but Bloch points out a close resemblance of this figure to the well-known Pompeian sculpture, *Dancing Satyr*. Paintings by William Sidney Mount and the Scotch artist David Wilkie had preceded Bingham's treatment of the rustic improvised dance, and their popularity encouraged him to explore this theme in his Missouri paintings.

Mercantile Library Collection

Sometimes a figure painted in shadow is clearly identified only in the drawing made for it, such as the tall man leaning against a barrel. The reclining man, leaning on his left elbow in the drawing, which McDermott suggests may have been done for the lost *Raftmen on the*

Ohio, has been reversed and otherwise adapted for this painting.

Mercantile Library Collection

Life on Missouri's Rivers

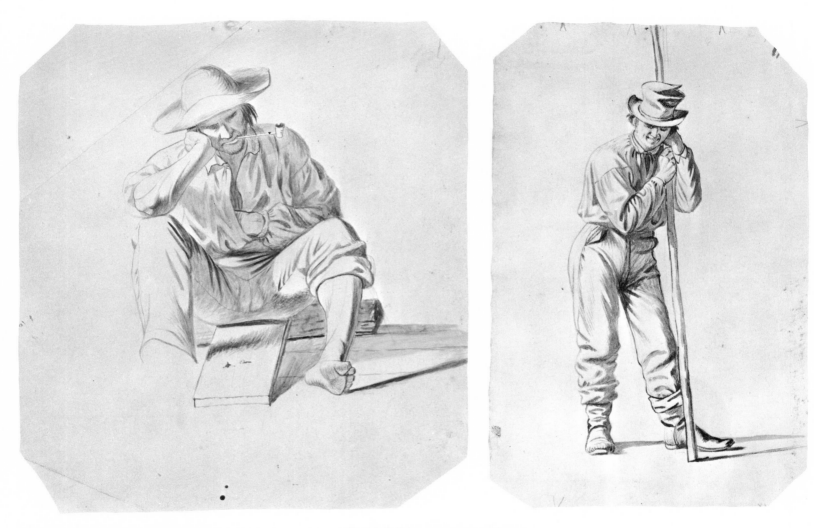

The man glumly contemplating a sore foot, who in this painting is dimly visible in the shadow of the barrel on the left side, was lifted with little revision from *Raftsmen Playing Cards* of 10 years earlier, in which he was painted in clear light. The man leaning on a pole (right) is a recurrent image, in several variations. In the shallow Missouri River poles kept the craft clear of sandbars; they had little use in the deep Mississippi channel.

Mercantile Library Collection

As Bingham acquired skill and confidence, he began turning his figures with involvements of foreshortening and perspective that he would not have dared to attempt a few years before. The figure seated in back view (left) is assured and well-poised. At right, the man seen in profile on the raft's deck.

Mercantile Library Collection

The man writing on a pad of paper, at right in the painting, is more like this drawing than like any similar figures in the election scenes, where he is obviously a newspaper man. Here he could be jotting down notes for one of the St. Louis papers, or he might be a riverfront dealer checking an invoice of delivered goods. In the drawing he is seated on a chair and is hatless. He and the townsman looking over his shoulder, and the two boys playing on the levee, are placed outside the highly contained composition on the raft. In the margin of this drawing is a separate study of a hand resting on a knee.

Mercantile Library Collection

Early Missourians and the Ballot

The Election Series

Missouri was granted statehood in 1821, after having already adopted a constitution and elected state officials. In the small river towns, where there was little public entertainment, the most general diversion was politics. Visits by candidates for office on speaking tours could be expected to attract sizeable and attentive audiences, and party rallies and conventions were occasions for militant speech-making, parades and street-corner debate.

There were two parties, the Whigs, ideological ancestors of today's Republicans, and Democrats. For some years the Whig term for a Democrat was "Locofoco." This curious word of uncertain origin has been tentatively traced to a self-lighting cigar with a built-in match invented by a New Yorker. At an 1835 meeting of a rump faction of New York City Democrats, the Tammany faction turned out the lights, and the meeting was conducted by the light of candles and locofocos.

After political feelings had built up like the steam pressure on a river boat, they were discharged in the grand excitement of election day. Only it was not one day, but three. "Elections in Missouri in the mid-nineteenth century were not conducted as they are today," McDermott explains in his book. "The ballot was not secret, precinct workers were not kept at a distance from the polls, and the voting lasted for three days. Elections were held viva voce, and a man could vote in any township

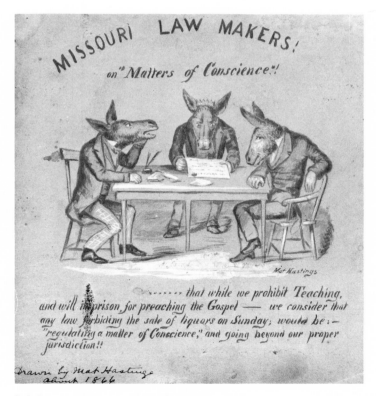

Subtlety was not a part of political persuasion as election time drew near. A depression of 1837 that was blamed on President Van Buren portrays him as a heavily clawed beast riding on the "Great Locofoco Juggernaut," and his predecessor, Andrew Jackson, in panel at right in what seems to be a travesty on the Liberty symbol. Below, a Mat Hastings cartoon showing Missouri lawmakers as donkeys. (Missouri Historical Society, St. Louis)

Early Missourians and the Ballot

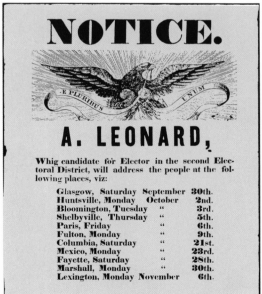

A crude election booth with a voter inside is overturned by a dissenter in the illustration from Leslie's Magazine of November 13, 1858 (top); the notice below invites audiences to speeches by a Whig candidate for elector in 1848.

in the county, but he had to swear that he had not and would not vote elsewhere. The voting scene, consequently, was far richer in variety of incident and character than it is in our time. This richness Bingham was to exploit fully.'' The election was followed, of course, by the tally of returns with more gatherings around the courthouses.

Bingham favored the Whig cause, and in 1844 with another election coming up and the convention scheduled for Boonville, he painted banners for the Boone, Cooper and Howard county delegations.

Bingham became increasingly active in politics. In 1846 he was elected to the Legislature from Saline County, but his opponent, E. D. Sappington, contested the vote and was awarded the position. A speech that Bingham made protesting the contest filled the entire front page of the *Missouri Statesman*, Columbia, in its issue of January 22, 1847. Two years later he defeated Sappington. Sarah Elizabeth Bingham died in 1848, and a year later he was married to Eliza K. Thomas, of Columbia.

In 1861 he was appointed a captain in the Volunteer Reserve Corps at Kansas City, which he had helped to organize, and the next year was appointed state treasurer to replace the incumbent, who had refused to take a loyalty oath. He was outspoken against secession, but he protested vehemently, in speeches and through his painting,

Order No. 11, against federal orders to evacuate the residents of Jackson, Bates, Cass and Vernon counties in over-reaction to raids by Kansas guerillas. In these years he continued to paint portraits and to add to his paintings of river and election themes.

He was a candidate for Congress in 1866, but was passed up by the nominating convention. By 1868 he had changed parties, and was chosen as an elector at the Democratic state convention. He moved to Independence, and almost immediately was elected school director. He had fallen out with the Art-Union, which was ordered disbanded soon afterward as a lottery, and he traveled about the country taking orders for engravings of his paintings.

He stayed in Independence a year, then moved to Kansas City, where he continued to work on portraits and his *Washington Crossing the Delaware*, an effort at grand style that like *Order No. 11* was not up to his Missouri subjects. He was appointed president of the Kansas City Board of Police Commissioners, and the next year, 1876, was appointed state adjutant-general. His second wife died in that year. When the University of Missouri established its School of Art, he was appointed a professor, while still traveling considerably and still painting. He was married for the third time in 1878, to Mrs. Martha Livingston Lykins of Kansas City. He died July 7, 1879.

Stump Speaking, 1853-1854   Oil on canvas, 42½ x 58   Boatmen's National Bank of
St. Louis

Early Missourians and the Ballot

In the large groups of his Election Series, Bingham achieved his finest and most ambitious compositions and characterizations. His assemblages of 50 or more figures are disposed seemingly at random, but actually are arranged with a tight unity of subgroups that contribute to the close-knit structure of the ensemble. Between the man standing to ask a question and the speaker responding with a fixed smile there is a push-pull tension that embraces the central part of the audience. The large man behind the speaker, obviously the rival candidate awaiting his turn, and the well-dressed man at right hold the outer elements together. The town drunk sits with glazed expression near the stand, and the audience abounds with other clear-cut types. It was sometimes proposed, or charged, that Bingham put recognizeable persons in his election groups. He once told a friend, however, that he had no particular persons in mind, at least for the major characters.

Detail from *Stump Speaking*

This painting is closely related to the lost *The Stump Orator* of 1847, known only through a daguerreotype, but is considerably more sophisticated in its placement of figures. The drawings of the speaker and the dubious distinguished citizen have a life of their own apart from their roles in the tableau.

The speaker is cast as a performer. His listeners were not necessarily won over in election-winning numbers by pure reason; the candidate had a stump and a crowd—and an opponent ready with his own performance. The better showman was likely to prevail.

Mercantile Library Collection

Early Missourians and the Ballot

Even a subordinate figure is carefully studied in the drawing. The man in the drawing, left, with details of costume and expression carefully worked out, is in the obscure lower left corner of the painting. The expression of the speaker's rival is changed from boredom in the drawing to a more irritated look in the painting.

Mercantile Library Collection

The boozy citizen and an amiable,
moon-faced listener (only their upper
torsos are visible in the painting) are
presented impartially and with good
humor, as are all the others gathered
to hear the speakers' words.

Early Missourians and the Ballot

Elderly attentive listener who, in the painting is seated just below the rustic lectern, and a boy who seems not to be listening. Since the boy is not facing the speaker, and hence not consciously imitating his finger-touching-palm gesture, the artist may have been, in this off-stage business, indulging in a bit of private drollery. The modeling of the foot displays a careful chiaroscuro —Bingham's early critics complained of a lack of this quality in his painting, and he took pains to remedy it.

Mercantile Library Collection

Canvassing For a Vote, 1851-1852   Oil on canvas, 25⅛ x 30³⁄₁₆   Nelson Gallery-Atkins Museum
(Nelson Fund, Kansas City)

Early Missourians and the Ballot

Another painting that was "lost" for a long time, in this case more than a century, and then found to have been not mislaid but on the wall of a private collection is *Canvassing For a Vote*, which Bingham completed in 1852 on commission from Goupil & Co., engravers. After a lithograph was made the painting passed from view, then turned up in Florida in 1954. The Nelson Gallery-Atkins Museum acquired it soon afterward.

Detail of *Canvassing For a Vote*

Both these figures can be recognized in *Canvassing For a Vote*, although each has gained a hat, and the fat man's pipe has been shifted to his left hand. The drawings had been used previously for the 1849 painting, *Country Politician*, which showed the group inside a tavern, and possibly for another similar painting, *Listening to the Wilmot Proviso*, which is known only through a description published in 1907. Bingham's fidelity to detail is seen in the politician's chair, a sturdy cane-seated ladderback of the kind made by country draftsmen.

Mercantile Library Collection

The listener who seems to be receptive to the canvasser's points has been made younger in the painting than in the preparatory drawing, but otherwise is almost duplicated. The Goupil lithograph, made by Claude Regnier, took unusual liberties with the original. It moved the group forward, cropped out considerable background, altered the position of the speaker, and sacrificed Bingham's descriptive treatment of the building; Bingham's forceful background tree and sky were routinely diluted.

Mercantile Library Collection

The County Election, Number Two,
1854

Line and mezzotint engraving,
hand-colored, 22 1/16 x 30 1/8

Collection, Governor and
Mrs. Christopher S. Bond.

Early Missourians and the Ballot

There are two *County Election* paintings, the first begun in 1851, worked on in Columbia and St. Louis and finished the next year; the second painted at Columbia in 1852. Both are in St. Louis collections, at the St. Louis Art Museum and Boatmen's Bank, respectively.

No. 1 was on loan to the Mercantile Library for several years, and was owned by the Library for a half-century before the museum purchased it in 1944.

No. 2 was taken on tour by Bingham as an inducement for print subscription orders. Robert J. Ward of Louisville bought it from him at New Orleans for $1,200. It was purchased by C. B. Rollins of Columbia and brought back to Missouri. The bank acquired it from Rollins's estate. John Sartain made an engraving from the first painting, but included some minor features that are only in the second, and this caused years of confusion, not yet positively resolved, as to which painting was actually first. Both McDermott and Bloch award priority to the museum version. Boatmen's Bank owns the steel plate from which the engravings were made.

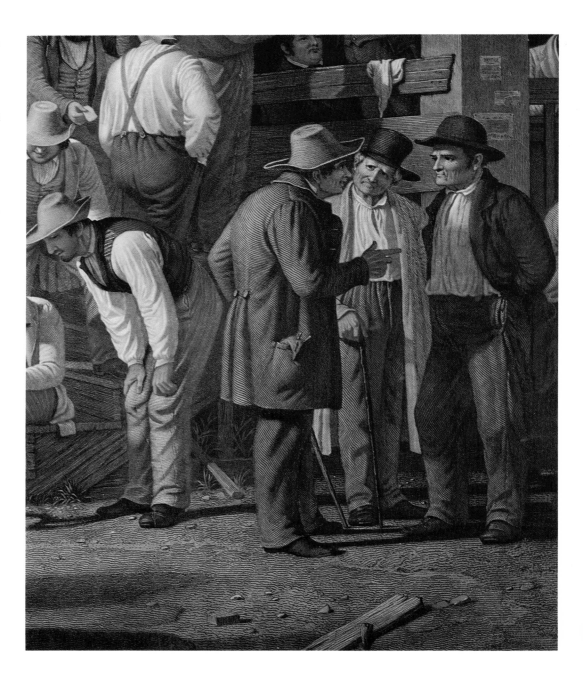

Detail from *County Election* engraving

Three men exchanging views near courthouse steps, composed in two drawings. In the museum's painting, there are two more men just beyond them, not included in *County Election No. 2* nor in the engraving reproduced here. Three quite different hat styles are seen in these studies, three varieties of long coat and shirts with collar bands.

Mercantile Library Collection

Early Missourians and the Ballot

A rather familiar feature of election day gatherings was the table provided, it may be conjectured, by a candidate with a sincere wish to serve the people. A popular refreshment was cider royal, a "concentrated" cider with honey added. Bingham portrays a sovereign giving thought to his election day responsibilities. The man serving was given a hat and an apron in the painting.

Mercantile Library Collection

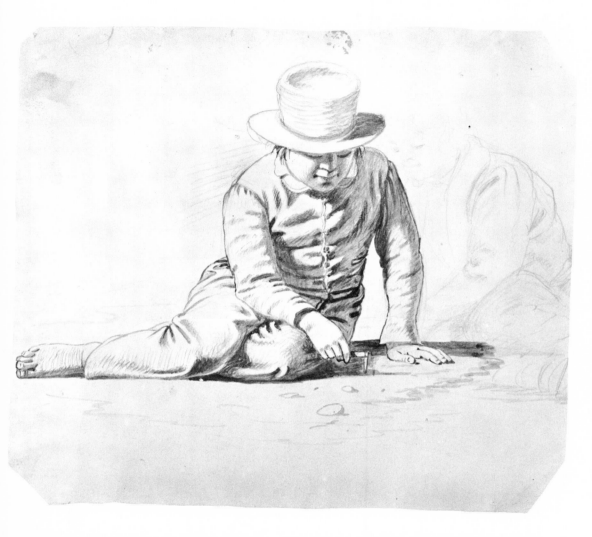

Bingham's second son, Horace, served as model for the boy playing mumble-the-peg, usually pronounced mumblety-peg. It was played by balancing a pocket knife on its half-open long blade and flipping it so as to make it land with its fully open short blade stuck in the ground, and scored by the straightness of the landing. The loser pulled up with his teeth a peg driven in the ground.

Mercantile Library Collection

Early Missourians and the Ballot

An earnest citizen in the two-figure group at left pokes his hand with a finger to emphasize the gravity of a pronouncement that he seems to be making. Bingham had by this time acquired skill at making a back view expressive, and the second man here appears to be listening calmly. The man with foot on the first step up to take his oath (right) has almost exactly this appearance in the museum's painting, but the hat brim obscures the face in the bank's painting and in the Sartain engraving.

Toothless ancient with numerals "76" on his hat crown comes down the steps. Only his head and shoulders are seen in the paintings, and his characterization has been somewhat softened. In the other drawing a "striker" (election worker) hands a card to a man who is next in line to take his oath and vote. In the paintings the striker is tipping his hat. Bingham painted many portraits of women, but there is not one woman in all the drawings of the Mercantile Library collection. Women are prominent in only three of his genre paintings, and each has the effect of a stock figure.

Mercantile Library Collection

Early Missourians and the Ballot

A diligent party worker who has won a vote and is struggling to deliver it has almost reached the polling place. Of the two studies that Bingham made for this situation, he used the pose at right for the party worker's head and attitude, but tidied up his hat. Causing him to face the courthouse porch gives him better unity with the composition. The voter being dragged to exercise his franchise is from the first drawing, with arms hanging limply.

Mercantile Library Collection

Books on Bingham

Bloch, E. Maurice, *George Caleb Bingham: A Catalogue Raisonne.* Berkeley and Los Angeles: University of California Press, 1967

Bloch, E. Maurice, *George Caleb Bingham: The Evolution of an Artist.* Berkeley and Los Angeles: University of California Press, 1967

Bloch, E. Maurice, *George Caleb Bingham 1811-1879.* An exhibition catalogue published for the National Collection of Fine Arts by Smithsonian Institution Press, Washington, D.C., 1968

Christ-Janer, Albert, *George Caleb Bingham: Frontier Painter of Missouri.* New York: Harry N. Abrams, 1975

Christ-Janer, Albert, *George Caleb Bingham of Missouri.* New York: Dodd, Mead, 1940

Constant, Alberta Wilson, *Paintbox on the Frontier: The Life and Times of George Caleb Bingham:* New York: Thomas Y. Crowell, 1974

Larkin, Lew, *Bingham: Fighting Artist. The Story of Missouri's Immortal Painter, Patriot, Soldier and Statesman.* St. Louis: State Publishing Co., 1955

McDermott, John Francis, *George Caleb Bingham: River Portraitist.* Norman, Okla.: University of Oklahoma Press, 1959

Rusk, Fern Helen, *George Caleb Bingham: The Missouri Artist.* Jefferson City, Mo.: The Hugh Stephens Co., 1917

Taggart, Ross E., "George Caleb Bingham Sesquicentennial Exhibition 1811-1961," *The Nelson Gallery and Atkins Museum Bulletin*, Vol. III, No. 3

Obligations

To John Francis McDermott and E. Maurice Bloch, for the painstaking research that provided most of the substance of this catalogue (see Books on Bingham).

To John Lindenbush, director of the Missouri Historical Society and Gail Guidry, picture librarian, for use of illustrations and research service.

To Richard Brownlee, director of the State Historical Society of Missouri, for illustrations.

For color transparencies: St. Louis Art Museum, Nelson Gallery-Atkins Museum, Boatmen's National Bank of St. Louis, Metropolitan Museum of Art, Governor Christopher S. Bond

Bingham's Missouri

Exhibition co-ordinator, Nancy Edelman
Catalogue by George McCue
Catalogue and poster design by Charles P. Reay

This catalogue set in 10 point Melior type by National Typographers, and printed on Quintessence Dull and Karma Natural Papers. Lithography by Sayers of Saint Louis.